Courting Disaster

A Comedy

Margaret Wood

Samuel French – London
New York – Sydney – Toronto – Hollywood

Copyright © 1983 by Samuel French Ltd
All Rights Reserved

COURTING DISASTER is fully protected under the copyright laws of the British Commonwealth, including Canada, the United States of America, and all other countries of the Copyright Union. All rights, including professional and amateur stage productions, recitation, lecturing, public reading, motion picture, radio broadcasting, television and the rights of translation into foreign languages are strictly reserved.

ISBN 978-0-573-12037-4

www.samuelfrench.co.uk
www.samuelfrench.com

For Amateur Production Enquiries

UNITED KINGDOM AND WORLD EXCLUDING NORTH AMERICA

plays@samuelfrench.co.uk

020 7255 4302/01

Each title is subject to availability from Samuel French, depending upon country of performance.

CAUTION: Professional and amateur producers are hereby warned that COURTING DISASTER is subject to a licensing fee. Publication of this play does not imply availability for performance. Both amateurs and professionals considering a production are strongly advised to apply to the appropriate agent before starting rehearsals, advertising, or booking a theatre. A licensing fee must be paid whether the title is presented for charity or gain and whether or not admission is charged.

The professional rights in this play are controlled by Samuel French Ltd, 24-32 Stephenson Way, London, NW1 2HD.

No one shall make any changes in this title for the purpose of production. No part of this book may be reproduced, stored in a retrieval system, or transmitted in any form, by any means, now known or yet to be invented, including mechanical, electronic, photocopying, recording, videotaping, or otherwise, without the prior written permission of the publisher. No one shall upload this title, or part of this title, to any social media websites.

The right of Margaret Wood to be identified as author of this work has been asserted in accordance with Section 77 of the Copyright, Designs and Patents Act 1988.

CHARACTERS
Meg, housekeeper
Sandra, her assistant
Trevor Lloyd, farmer
PC Bowen, beloved of Sandra
Hughie, Trevor's youngest brother
Phoebe Hunter, eligible neighbouring spinster
Alice Chapman, eligible widow

The action takes place in a farmhouse kitchen/living-room

Time — the present

COURTING DISASTER

A farmhouse kitchen/living-room. Morning

In the back wall LC *there is a door, which opens half-way, like a stable door. When the top half is open, the gable end of a barn can be seen outside.* R *of the door is a sideboard, and* DR *there is a kitchen table and chairs. Half-way down the wall* R *is a door to the rest of the house. Along the wall* L, *there is a sink and draining-board and a cooker.* DL, *facing the audience, is a settle (or, failing that, two chairs), with a small table in front of it and a mirror hanging above it*

When the CURTAIN *rises, Sandra, who is about twenty, is making pastry, sniffing and weeping into the bowl. Meg, about thirty, is at the sink, noisily washing pots and banging saucepans as if in annoyance, looking impatiently over her shoulder at Sandra as she does so. After a few seconds, she flicks the water off her hands and picks up a tea-towel*

Meg That pastry will be as heavy as lead, my girl, with you weeping into it like a waterfall.
Sandra I can't help it. (*She rolls out the pastry viciously*)
Meg And don't lean on it with the full weight of your grief.

She crosses to the table as Sandra sniffs and wipes her hand across her nose

And don't put that hand back in the bowl!! (*She smacks it*) Go and wash it. In *cold* water, for goodness sake. You need cool hands for pastry.

Sandra crosses sulkily to the sink

Tears of stricken love they may be, but they're unhygienic for all that.
Sandra Things like hygiene never enter a full heart.
Meg Never mind your full heart. Let it enter your empty head.

There is a pause while Sandra dries her hands and Meg sits at the table and begins peeling potatoes

PC Bowen again, I suppose. What's he done this time?

Sandra It's what he hasn't done. He never turned up to take me to the midsummer dance last night.

Meg Promised, had he?

Sandra N—no. But he knew I was going. (*She attacks the pastry again*)

Meg Policemen can't be at your beck and call all the time, girl. For all you know terrorists might have raided the post office, and PC Bowen was busy rounding them up.

Sandra (*with a fresh burst*) No he wasn't. He came to the dance all right—with that red-headed Marie Owen,

Meg (*scornfully*) Marie Owen? Pooh. Very temporary that will be. She gulps down men like a sewage disposal tank. There's an SAS group camping on the mountain next week. The police force will hold no further attractions for Marie Owen then.

Sandra (*fitting pastry over a tin*) I don't want her leavings.

Meg So what are you crying about, then?

Sandra (*hopefully*) Do you really think it'll be temporary?

Meg Certain. Put the kettle on and cheer up.

Sandra does so

The top half of the door bangs open and Trevor looks in—a tyrannical man with a good opinion of himself

Trevor Where's Hugh, then?

Meg (*without looking round*) Haven't seen him since breakfast, Mr Trevor. You told him to bale twenty-acre field, so I expect that's where he is.

Trevor Thought he'd have done that by now. (*He comes in and crosses to the settle* DL, *sits and starts removing his wellingtons*) Slow as a cart-horse, that brother of mine. Always was.

Meg (*sharply*) Steady as a cart-horse, too. Never leaves a job half done.

Trevor Pah! I could've finished baling that hay half an hour since.

Meg So you say.

Trevor Shoes. Where's my shoes?

Meg rises, fetches his shoes from under the sideboard, brings them to him, then takes his wellingtons and puts them outside the door

Now, Meg. Pay attention. I'll be wanting that jacket I told you to put away special.

Meg (*vaguely*) Jacket? I don't remember you mentioning any jacket.
Trevor (*impatiently*) It's not *any* jacket. It's my special jacket — I told you so when you first came here, didn't I?
Meg When I first came? Ten years ago? That's a long time to remember even something special, Mr Trevor.
Trevor (*pausing in tying his shoelaces and wagging a finger at her*) Special I said and special I meant. I said to you at the time, "If ever I find a moth in this here coat," I said, "you're fired!"
Meg (*returning to the table*) Oh, that one.
Trevor Yes, that one. You go and get it out and if it isn't perfect, I'll be as good as my word. (*Rising*) I'll be back for coffee at eleven.
Meg (*incredulously*) Coffee?
Trevor Yes, coffee. And there'll be an extra one — p'raps two. Only I've asked the second to come a bit later than the first.
Meg So it's a running buffet you'll be wanting, is it?
Trevor (*pointing his finger warningly*) No cheek from you, girl. Just have that jacket ready when I come back, see?

He goes out through the back door, leaving the top half open

Sandra What a fuss! What's so special about an old jacket, anyway?
Meg (*pausing in her potato peeling*) I wonder ... Judging by what I heard last night and what I've heard just now, I reckon we're in for some big changes
Sandra Why? What did you hear last night?
Meg (*looking over her shoulder cautiously*) Mr Trevor and his brother Hughie had a flaming row.
Sandra *Hughie* had a row? I thought he was too much under his brother's thumb to dare. (*Sniffing*) Too meek and mild in my opinion, is Hughie.
Meg (*sharply*) Your opinion isn't worth having, my girl. And it's *Mister* Hughie to you. (*Softly*) A man in a million, is Hughie.
Sandra (*coolly*) Fancy. I'd have missed him in a crowd of six. (*She begins filling the pastry case with jam*) *Why* is Hughie so soft? Mr Trevor treats him as if he's still a kid, with no mind of his own.
Meg (*sighing*) Hughie was only a kid of six when his father died. Trevor was seventeen. When there's that much difference in age, you get in the habit of doing what big brother tells you. Hughie's

not soft — just convinced that Trevor is the business genius on this farm and that he's the opposite.

Sandra If grabbing whatever you can get and being as mean as hell is business, Trevor's a genius all right.

Meg (*taking potatoes to the sink*) Yes. It's land, land, land first, second and last with Trevor. All head and no heart.

Sandra (*mischievously*) And Mr Hughie?

Meg (*softly; off her guard*) Hughie's all heart. (*She smiles to herself, then pulls up and turns sharply back to the table*) But his head's screwed on all right. He just hasn't any confidence, that's all.

Sandra (*pouncing*) You're sweet on him. (*She points at Meg across the table*) I always thought you were.

Meg (*smacking her hand down*) Stop shaking flour all over the place.

Sandra You are, you are! You're sweet on him! Now then. Tell me what the row was about.

Meg Well ... I don't know that I ought.

Sandra Oh, go on. You've started so you may as well finish — like Mastermind. What was it?

Meg I'm not *quite* sure. That door (*jerking her head to* R) is terrible thick and there's no keyhole, see? Not that I was listening, mind.

Sandra Course not. Go on. What did you hear?

Meg Well Hughie was saying, "You'll never get anyone as good as Meg to run the house, Trevor. You don't know when you're well off."

Sandra There now! And they say eavesdroppers never hear any good of themselves. What did the master say?

Meg He said, "You're a fool, Hugh. Meg's all right, but she hasn't got four hundred acres of fine farmland lying alongside mine, has she?" And he bangs the table — so — to show his feelings.

Sandra I don't see anything to bang about. What did he mean?

Meg Work it out, Sandra, work it out. Whose got four hundred acres on the east side of this farm?

Sandra (*vaguely*) East ... ? (*She puts out her hands like a scarecrow and revolves till she decides which is east*) East ... oh, yes. Old Mr Hunter's. But he's dead.

Meg Dead these eight months. But he has a daughter, hasn't he? Left her the farm and a stable full of horses. That's what Mr Trevor's after.

Sandra Phoebe Hunter? ... Bit long in the tooth, isn't she? Bit like a horse herself.

Meg Looks aren't what the master's after. Land is his light of love.
Sandra What if she won't have him?
Meg Just what Hughie asked last night. And I gathered that if Trevor can't get what lies on one side of his farm, he'll try the other.
Sandra You mean Mrs Alice Chapman? A married lady?
Meg Widowed, Sandra, widowed. And all the more attractive for that. Only three hundred acres instead of five, but a tidy bank balance, a big house and good antique furniture. Kettle's boiling its head off. (*She crosses to the stove and makes tea*)

Hughie appears at the half-door and pauses to take off his wellingtons. He is about thirty. He reacts to Sandra's next words

Sandra So he's got two to choose from. There's big thinking for you! Hemmed in by eligible ladies. Which do you think he'll have?
Meg Which do you think will have *him*?
Hughie (*coming in*) That's what worries me.
Sandra Oh, Mr Hughie. You made me jump.
Hughie Trevor not back yet?
Meg Been and gone. Back at eleven. Got time to have a cup of tea before they come? (*She brings the pot to the table*)
Hughie They?
Sandra He said there's be an extra one for coffee—p'raps two.
Hughie (*dropping into the chair* R *of the table*) My God!
Meg No. Only Phoebe Hunter or Alice Chapman. Pour out, Sandra. I've got to get that jacket. And put the kettle on again. It'll have to be instant coffee. We haven't any real stuff.

Meg exits, R

Sandra puts on the kettle and brings cups to the table

Hughie Beats me how you women always know what's in the wind. Moles in M.I.5 have nothing on you. How do you two know what Trevor has in mind?
Sandra (*pouring tea*) Those that have ears to hear, jolly well listen. There's your tea. If Mr Trevor will discuss his matrimonial intentions as if he were reciting at the Eisteddfod in a force-eight gale, he must expect Meg to give it due care and attention.
Hughie I don't think he's serious. He's teasing me, that's all.
Sandra Maybe. But Phoebe Hunter's coming to coffee, isn't she?

Hughie You don't know that. It may be a man.

Sandra (*sitting L of the table with her tea*) Elevenses for men means beer: elevenses for Meg and me means tea and we have it at half-past ten: elevenses with *coffee* means ladies. Besides, he's changed into shoes and asked for his special jacket.

Hughie What jacket?

Meg enters R, carrying a jacket

Meg (*as she enters*) His special jacket. His *courting* jacket. (*She shakes it out*)

Sandra Pooh—what a stink!

Hughie You don't mean to say he's *bought* a jacket? Must have been to Oxfam.

Meg Not at all. Even an Oxfam one wouldn't smell like this. Sentimental about this jacket, is Trevor. (*She puts it over the back of the centre chair*) When I first came here, ten years ago, just after his wife died, he showed that coat to me. "See here, girl," he said, "I wore this jacket when I was courting my Dilys, and if ever I find a moth's been at it, you're fired!!"

Sandra That's lovely. Really romantic, that is.

Meg H'm. He added, "I might need it again at any moment, so see to it." (*She sits and sips her tea*)

Sandra He's waited for ten years, though.

Hughie He waited for old Hunter or old Chapman to die, you mean. They've both obliged at last.

Meg It was such a close finish that he's got a choice. Another cup, Hughie?

Hughie Might as well. I'll get a rocket if he finds me here and I'll get a rocket if he doesn't ... I don't know what to do next, see? He said bale twenty-acre field and I have. Do I go on to thirty-acre, or wait for him to say?

Meg (*suddenly aware of Sandra*) Sandra, take those potato peelings to the swill tub and pick some raspberries on the way back.

Sandra Oh Meg! I haven't had a second cup yet.

Meg There's a bowl on the side. Pick plenty. There's no hurry.

Sandra (*collecting the peelings and a bowl from the sideboard*) I hate picking raspberries: and I wanted to see what happens at coffee time.

She goes off into the farmyard disconsolately, closing the door behind her

Hughie (*gloomily*) Praps I'd better start on thirty-acre.
Meg Hughie, for heaven's sake make a decision for yourself for once. If it's ready for baling, bale it.
Hughie Trevor'll only say I'm high-handed. Ask me who the hell I think I am.
Meg BE high-handed. *Tell* him who you are. Stand up to him as you did last night. And talking of that, thank you for those kind words you spoke to Trevor about me. He never notices anything I do to make life more comfortable or easy for him.
Hughie (*eagerly*) *I* notice, Meg. I think you're a right wonder, Meg. Always looked up to you, I have, ever since you first came.
Meg (*sighing*) That's what you always do, Hughie—look *up* to people. Why can't you look *at* them, on your own level—as you're looking at me now. (*Tenderly*) You're as good as anyone I know—better in fact.

They look at each other for a few moments: then Hughie looks away sheepishly

Hughie Ah, no, Meg. Exaggerating you are. I'll always be second fiddle.
Meg (*passionately*) But you could be first fiddle! If only you made up your mind to it, you could be... oh, you could be conductor of the whole orchestra!

She puts her hand on his; he looks at her. There is a pause. Then a knock on the door

Damn!

The top half opens to reveal PC Bowen

(*Rising*) Good-morning, PC Bowen. And what would you be wanting this time? Have we been driving tractors to the danger or is swine fever sweeping the country?
Bowen (*entering the kitchen and looking round unhappily*) Er... no. I'm just checking that Mr Trevor's gun licence is in order.
Meg (*following him* DS) Do you think I'm simple, PC Bowen? You came to see if Sandra's in order didn't you? Well, she's not. I'm surprised at you, David Bowen, I really am, turning up at a dance with that red-headed Salome of the seven veils from Orcop.
Bowen It wasn't my fault, Miss Davis, really it wasn't. She hooked me at the door and wouldn't let go.
Meg (*sitting at the table and pouring tea into Sandra's cup*) Call

yourself a policeman and you get arrested at the door by a plastic face with false eyelashes. Here, have a cup of tea. You won't mind having Sandra's cup? (*She hands him the cup*)

Bowen Indeed no, Miss Davis. It will be a pleasure. (*He sips it lovingly*) I was weak, you see, Miss Davis. I *am* weak. I didn't want to offend anyone, and I offended Sandra, who is the last person I wanted to upset, and I couldn't catch her eye all evening because she was always looking the other way, and——

Meg I should think she was! You and that scarlet runner of a beanpole couldn't have been a pretty sight. (*She pauses, then softens at the sight of his misery*) Well, if you want to catch her eye now, she's in the raspberry canes, behind the barn.

Bowen (*hastily depositing the cup*) Oh, thank you, Miss Davis, thank you. (*He turns to the door*)

Meg (*smiling to herself*) Good place for courting, the raspberry canes. Nice and high this year.

Bowen (*pulling down his jacket and returning to his official manner*) I'll – er – proceed to the spot immediately. Thank you for helping me with my enquiries, Miss Davis.

PC Bowen exits

Meg (*indulgently*) Well, it might improve her pastry. Look at it. Like a bit of damp plaster. Bung it in the oven and say a prayer for the poor thing. (*She does so*) What are you laughing at, Hughie?

Hughie By damn, you're a proper caution, Meg. Even got the arm of the law under your thumb.

Meg It's nice to hear you laughing, Hughie. Real old worryguts you are this morning.

Hughie Of course I'm worried. What are *you* going to do if Trevor marries either of those harpies?

Meg I'm not worried. I shan't be here to welcome the bride.

Hughie Oh, but he wants you to stay on, Meg. He says he can afford a housekeeper when he's got a rich wife and twice the amount of land.

Meg I daresay. He wants a housekeeper so that Phoebe can devote herself to her horses and hunting, or Alice Chapman can do her flower arranging, WI, meals-on-wheels and drama club just as if she was still a merry widow.

Hughie No wonder her poor old husband upped and died.

Malnutrition, I should think. He wasn't entitled to meals-on-wheels, see?

They laugh

Meg Fair play, she did the flowers beautiful for the funeral. (*Seriously*) Hughie, what are *you* going to do if Trevor marries?
Hughie I don't know. Came on me like a bombshell. Last night I told him I wouldn't stay. "Go then," he says. "Go and live in the gamekeeper's cottage that Father left you and see how you like it."

There is a pause

Meg I always thought that gamekeeper's cottage had possibilities: nice situation, facing south over my old Uncle Gareth's land and——
Hughie Aw, no. It's been empty since old Beynon died. The roof leaks, the window frames are all warped, there's dry rot under the sink; and only an earth closet down the garden.
Meg A double one, though. Very companionable if you like a social life.

Into the laughter bursts an angry Trevor from the farmyard

Hughie rises guiltily

Trevor I thought as much. Sitting on your arse drinking tea and having a giggle while I do all the work. What the hell do you think you're up to, wasting my time and money?
Meg He's finished twenty-acre field and came to ask you what to do next.
Trevor Start on thirty-acre of course, you dolt.

Trevor exits R

Hughie Can't win, can I?
Meg (*pushing him back in his chair*) Finish your tea, Hughie. Baling's thirsty work.
Hughie No, no. I've finished. I'm off. (*He goes to the door*)
Meg Hughie.

Hughie turns

I shouldn't worry too much. Trevor won't be getting married.
Hughie What makes you think that?

Meg (*piling up cups*) I took him at his word about that jacket. It's been in mothballs for ten years. No woman would let him get near enough to pop the question.
Hughie (*laughing*) But won't he notice it?
Meg No. There's one thing to be said for broiler houses after all, Hughie. If you work in them long enough, you can't tell a manure heap from a lily of the valley. (*She takes the cups to the sink*)
Hughie My saints! You're a marvel, Meg.
Meg Off with you, he's coming.

Hughie exits into the farmyard, leaving the half-door open

Trevor enters R, *his face in a towel*

Trevor (*as he enters*) Got that jacket?
Meg On the chair. (*She goes to the sideboard and puts out two cups, a jug of milk, sugar and a jar of instant coffee on a tray*)
Trevor (*flicking back his hair with a comb and inspecting the jacket*) H'm. Looks all right. (*He puts it on*) Smells a bit musty but that'll soon air itself off. (*He surveys himself in the mirror over the settle*) Ha! How's that for a fit? Not an ounce have I put on in the last ten years. See that, Meg? There's a figure for you. That's what hard work does. No sitting and drinking tea half the morning for me.
Meg Hughie works just as hard as you and is just as slim. (*She goes back to the sideboard and pauses by the half-open door. Innocently*) Well, good gracious, now! There's Miss Phoebe Hunter riding into the yard. Whatever can she want?

Trevor agitatedly straightens his tie, sits in a chair and opens a newspaper, trying to look at ease. There is a clatter of hooves and a woman's horsey voice, off

Phoebe (*off*) Steady there. Steady old girl. That's it.
Trevor (*in an agitated whisper*) I told you there'd be company for coffee. Get on with it, woman.

Phoebe appears at the half-door

Phoebe Well, here I am, Trevor, as requested. (*She looks down at the door*) What am I supposed to do with this fence? Jump it?
Trevor (*rising hastily*) No, no. I'll unlatch it. Come in. Sit down, Miss Hunter. Sit down ...

Phoebe comes down, looking round at Meg and the kitchen, puts her riding-crop on the small table and sits on the settle

And give us that coffee, girl. Then clear out.

Meg (*dumping the tray on the table and pouring water into the cups*) Milk's in jug. Sugar's in bowl.

She returns the kettle to the stove and exits R *without a backward glance*

Phoebe (*watching her with haughty disapproval*) You should snaffle that filly short and keep her on a tight rein, Trevor my lad; she has a very defiant manner. Needs breaking in.

Trevor Aw she's a good housekeeper.

Phoebe What? When she spoons instant coffee into cups and serves it with cold milk? You don't know how things should be done, Trevor. Perhaps you never did.

Trevor Now look here, Miss Hunter——

Phoebe I *am* looking. It's simply not done, you know, to ask a lady to coffee and serve it in the kitchen. (*Sniffing*) And there's something wrong with your drains. Can't you smell it? (*She takes her coffee cup*)

Trevor (*leaning across her to get his*) Smell what?

Phoebe Good God! It's enough to knock you out! I can't smell the coffee for the . . . the camphor! That's what it is. It's not drains, it's camphor. It's goddam awful.

Trevor (*irritated*) Look, forget the bloody smell. I asked you here to listen to a proposition.

Phoebe Well get on with it, man. Don't beat about the bush while I gasp for air.

Trevor Well. (*He edges closer*) Phoebe, my dear. It's a bit delicate like——

Phoebe Rubbish. You're not a delicate man. Out with it.

Trevor I've been thinking, Phoebe. You must be very lonely since your father died. (*He leans closer*)

Phoebe My God! It's getting worse! I really can't stand——(*She takes out her hanky*)

Trevor (*seizing the free hand*) I'm a very lonely man, Phoebe. We're two lonely people . . . (*He looks expectantly at her*) Well, can't you see what I'm getting at?

Phoebe shakes her head dumbly

Two lonely people should get together. Get wed.

Phoebe (*withdrawing her hand sharply*) Lonely? *I'm* not lonely. I've got my horses and farm and a good income. I enjoy life.

Trevor But it's not the same as having a man about the house, is it?

Phoebe By God, it's not. It's a damn sight better.

Trevor But look—I could advise you about the farm and the stables and horses and share my home with you. You'd be a different woman, Phoebe.

Phoebe I'd damn well have to be to say yes to that set-up. (*Rising*) I can manage my own affairs just as well as you can and ... (*She pauses and sniffs around him*) By heaven—it's YOU! Is that your idea of aftershave or what? Let me tell you, Mr Trevor Mothballs, if I marry, it'll be someone who doesn't stink worse than a dog fox.

Trevor (*rising, equally enraged*) Come to that, *you* smell of the stables. Living with you would be like sharing a loose box with a brood mare.

Phoebe (*striking the table with her crop and making as if to strike him*) You ... you——

Meg pokes her head round the door R

Meg (*sweetly*) Can I get you any more coffee, Miss Hunter?

Trevor (*violently*) Get out, you. GET OUT!

Meg grins and disappears

Phoebe (*breathing deeply and seizing Trevor by his tie*) God forbid that I should strike a mere man, Trevor Lloyd, but much more from you and you'll feel this crop across your withers. Out of my way! (*She pushes him aside, giving him a whack across his bottom as she strides to the door. She goes through and turns to face him over the lower half for her parting shot*) And while we're having this delicate talk about propositions, what about cleaning out that pond on your lower pasture? It breeds mosquitoes and it stinks—like its owner.

Trevor (*advancing on her*) WOMAN! Get out, get out.

Phoebe exits

Meg enters sunnily, R

Meg Well, that was a very short visit. (*Taking the tray*) She hasn't even finished her coffee.

Trevor Women. Bloody women! Get me some whisky.
Meg Sure? There's plenty of coffee in your cup too. (*She puts the tray on the draining-board then goes to the sideboard and fetches a whisky*)
Trevor That — that female there is practically a horse herself. She laid back her ears, curled her lip over her buck teeth and rolled her eyes — she'd have reared up on her hind legs if she hadn't been on 'em already.
Meg What *could* have upset her? (*She gives him the whisky*)
Trevor Your way of serving coffee for one. What the hell did you bring it in like that for? You never have before. (*He swigs whisky*)
Meg I thought it would bring out the worst in Miss Phoebe. I didn't want you to buy a pig in a poke.
Trevor And another thing. You've made me into some kind of polecat, you have. (*Taking off his jacket*) It stinks, she said.
Meg Well now. You didn't give me much notice, did you? Two days at least in the open air that jacket needed, but you wanted it sudden and special——
Trevor (*irritably*) Hang it on the line now. And get me another whisky.
Meg (*going to the back door*) It's Hughie's whisky.
Trevor So much the better.

Meg goes off into the yard to hang the jacket on the line

Meg (*off*) Well, we *are* popular this morning. There's Miss Phoebe going and Mrs Alice Chapman coming.
Trevor Aw, hell! (*He goes to the sideboard and helps himself to a quick whisky*) Are they talking to each other?
Meg (*off*) Not sure. Miss Phoebe's looking down from her horse and roaring with laughter——

Trevor swallows his whisky with one gulp

—and Mrs Chapman's looking up at her, puzzled-like.

Meg comes in and shuts the door

Am I to make more coffee?
Trevor Yes. And do it properly this time.
Meg Oh, I've done it. It's on the table in the dining-room, silver set and all. Different people need different methods.

Meg exits R

There is a knock on the door. Trevor goes to it

Trevor Ah, Mrs Chapman, come in and sit down.

Alice Chapman enters

(*A thought striking him*) Or would you prefer the sitting-room?

Alice (*briskly, business-like*) No, no. I always do my business in the kitchen. The right working atmosphere I think. (*She sits on the settle*). It *was* business, wasn't it?

Trevor Well, in a manner of speaking. There's a softer side to it than just business, though.

Meg enters R with coffee in a silver set. She places it in front of them

Meg Morning, Mrs Chapman. Will you have black or white?

Alice Just a touch of milk, please. (*She picks up the sugar-bowl and surreptitiously inspects it*)

Meg It's all right. It *is* hall-marked. So is the pot and the milk jug.

Alice replaces the bowl sharply

Your coffee, Mrs Chapman. And yours, Mr Trevor. Call me if you want anything more.

Meg exits R

Alice (*sipping her coffee reflectively and looking round*) What's all this in aid of, Trevor? Best silver out for morning coffee on a Tuesday? Who are you trying to impress?

Trevor (*airily*) Oh, I leave all that sort of thing to Meg. I expect she needed a clean jug, seeing that we'd just had coffee with—er—that we'd just had coffee.

Alice Oh, so Phoebe's been to coffee, has she? Do you know what she said when she passed me just now?

Trevor (*nervously*) N—no. Something horsey, I bet.

Alice I don't know. P'raps it was. She said "Here comes the second string", and burst out laughing. Can't imagine what she meant. (*Suddenly looking at him*) Or perhaps I can. What's this business proposition of yours?

Trevor Well, it's not so much a business proposition as an affair of the heart, Alice.

Alice In your case they probably mean the same thing. Come on. Make up your mind. Business proposal, marriage proposal or both?

Trevor (*taken aback*) Well ... if you put it like that, a bit of both. (*Moving closer, sentimentally*) You're a sensible, practical woman, Alice, my dear. You can see the advantages, can't you? Two lonely people——
Alice (*nodding*) *And* two large farms, two lots of outbuildings, agricultural machinery, stock ... Oh yes, indeed. (*Eyeing him narrowly*) What did Phoebe Hunter say to it?
Trevor That woman? Do you think I'd give her the chance?
Alice (*drily*) Yes. She's got more land than I have. *And* horses.
Trevor But I don't want horses. I want you, Alice. What do you say?
Alice (*leaning back and eyeing him speculatively*) I'd have to consider ...
Trevor Consider away, my dear. But when we're married, I'll do the considering for you. You won't have to bother your little head about business any more.
Alice (*firmly*) My little head is a very good little head for business. It's no bother. Who do you think ran the farm when my husband was alive? Not him, oh dear no. He couldn't sow a row of peas straight. The farm's mine and always has been.
Trevor Ours, Alice. Ours.
Alice Mine, Trevor, MINE. I shall continue to run it and you can come and live in my house, which is a deal more comfortable than this, and your brother Hugh can move in here.
Trevor Look, who's making these arrangements—you or me? I don't want Hughie moving in here——
Alice (*over-riding him*) My second condition is that we have separate banking accounts. That way we don't get in a muddle. Your debts are yours and mine are mine.
Trevor But the profits, Alice, the profits! What about the profits from a big concern? At least consider a joint account.
Alice (*adamantly*) Separate accounts at separate banks.
Trevor Well, damn that——
Alice The third condition is——
Trevor (*exploding*) Bugger your conditions! Do you think I'm marrying you just to get a bed in your house? What's in it for me? You can keep your farm and your separate banking account—and I hope it's in the red by the time the harvest's over.
Alice (*rising placidly*) My account will still be in the black, even if the harvest's as big a wash-out as your matrimonial plans.

Goodbye, Trevor Lloyd, and better hunting with your next! (*She goes to the door*)

Meg enters R

Meg Oh, Mrs Chapman, you haven't finished already, have you?

Alice exits

Can't I get you anything else?

Trevor (*sitting, disgusted, at the table*) Don't stop her, Meg. Don't stop her. She makes more conditions than a trade union.

Meg (*closing the door behind Alice*) Goodbye for now, then, Mrs Chapman. Be seeing you some day I expect.

Trevor Don't you dare see that old bitch.

Meg (*clearing the coffee things*) Would you believe it? She's not drunk her coffee either. Nor you. We've got a surplus of this stuff, you know.

Trevor Conditions! I offer her marriage and she offers me conditions!

Meg Well, she's in a position to do so, isn't she? An independent woman like her?

Trevor (*banging the table*) Well, I don't hold with it, Meg my girl. Not at all. If a woman loves a man, she freely and willingly with all her worldly goods does with him share. Isn't that right?

Meg No, it isn't. It's the man who promises that. (*She picks up the tray*) It's the first lie every bridegroom tells his bride. (*Coming to the table*) And who's talking about love, anyway? Alice doesn't give a rap for you, nor you for her.

Trevor (*angrily*) Cheeky you are getting, Meg. I've had enough of it. Talking to me as if you were my superior.

Meg (*setting down the tray with a bang*) Face facts, Trevor. I am.

Trevor (*staggered; rising*) Who the hell are you calling Trevor? *Mister* Trevor to you. Don't you mix me up with my milksop brother that you're so familiar with. Hughie's never had any sense of the dignity or respect due to his position.

Meg (*coming round the front of the table to confront him*) He's no need to. Hughie has the respect of everyone. When I came here first, ten years ago, Hughie and I were both youngsters. I called him Hughie and no-one thought he'd lost any dignity. If people are polite to you it's because you're a bully, not because of your

"position". They dislike you, but they love Hughie. (*She is nearly in tears as she finishes*)
Trevor (*crossing, enraged, to the settle*) Love? Pah! There's no profit in love.
Meg How do you know? You've never tried it. And while we are talking straight, *Mister* Trevor, I'm giving you notice. A week. (*She takes up the tray and moves to the sink*)
Trevor A week? You can't do that!
Meg I can. You pay me by the week. I give a week's notice.

The back door opens and Sandra enters, shining-eyed, carrying the raspberry bowl. PC Bowen stands outside the door, as Sandra turns and kisses him over the half-door. PC Bowen exits

Trevor, who is staring stupefied before him, notices nothing of this

Sandra Oh, Meg. My pastry will be as light as my heart in future.
Meg (*drily*) That'll be a nice change. You've taken your time over those raspberries.
Sandra (*coyly*) Well, I was delayed by someone. (*She puts the bowl on the draining-board*)
Trevor Stop nattering, you hen-witted women. You can't give notice, Meg. Who'd run the house?
Meg A good question, Trevor. Yes. Who's going to do the sweeping, the baking, the bed-making, the washing, ironing, window-cleaning, shoe-cleaning, orders for the butcher, the baker, the candlestick maker, the dinner by one o'clock, the supper by seven and all the rest of it? I hoped it would be Phoebe the Filly or Alice the Bitch. As it is, you'll have to make do with Sandra here.
Sandra (*appalled*) Hey, wait a minute, Meg. I'm not doing all that. Besides, I'm getting married next spring.
Trevor (*to Sandra*) Get out, GET OUT!!

Sandra flees R

(*Turning to Meg*) Now, my girl. Have a bit of sense. Calm down and get me another whisky.
Meg (*clearing the table of cooking things*) Not I. You've had enough of Hughie's whisky
Trevor (*placatory*) Well, p'raps you're right. Now. Listen quietly. How old are you?

Meg How old are *you*?

Trevor That's none of your business.

Meg Then mine is none of yours.

Trevor Well, you're not in your first bloom, are you?

Meg (*quietly*) Some of us bloom late. Perhaps I'm one.

Trevor What I mean is, where will you get another job? There'll be no reference from me if you quit, I can tell you that. You like it here, don't you?

Meg (*taking a tablecloth from the sideboard drawer*) For some things—and some people.

Trevor Then don't be hasty. You've no living relatives, have you?

Meg Not since my Uncle Gareth died last month. I'm alone.

Hughie comes to the half-door

Trevor Then be practical, girl. Don't go giving in your notice just because you're jealous of those two women. Don't think I didn't see through your tricks to put them off me.

Meg (*amazed*) Jealous? (*She claps her hand over her mouth in derision and laughter*)

Hughie (*coming in; appalled*) Notice? Who's giving notice?

Trevor Meg. Pay no attention. She doesn't mean it. It's just temper.

Trevor flings out through the back door

Hughie (*sitting L of the table, stunned*) Oh, Meg. You've never given notice!

Meg Why not? I told you I should. (*She fetches cutlery*)

Hughie (*brightening*) But there's no need. I've just seen Alice Chapman. They both turned him down

Meg I'm still leaving. (*She begins to put out cutlery on the table*)

Hughie But why? . . . And what did he mean about being jealous? Oh, my saints! Is it *Trevor* you're in love with?

Meg (*ridiculing*) Trevor? (*Then seeing an opportunity, she alters her course of action and adopts a coquettish air*) What if I am? Anything against it?

Hughie N--n . . . I mean, I never guessed . . . from the way you talked . . .

Meg I don't wear my heart on my sleeve. (*Bitterly*) If I did I doubt anyone would notice it. (*She bangs down knives and forks*)

Hughie (*facing the audience, elbows on knees, despairingly*) So it was Trevor all the time.

Meg (*faltering*) All what time?
Hughie All the time I was thinking ... hoping it might be ... well, someone else. (*Hastily*) I never thought it could be, mind, but——
Meg (*tremulously — holding out her hand towards him*) Oh, Hughie, I didn't mean——
Hughie Trevor's a good catch, mind!
Meg (*slamming down the final spoon in despair*) Depends who's fishing. Trevor's out for a whale. I'm only a sprat. (*She fetches side-plates*)
Hughie (*sadly*) I'm only a sprat, too. I think that's why I've always felt so comfortable with you, Meg. I can tell you anything.
Meg (*savagely*) I wish you would.
Hughie When our dad died, Trevor was a lot older than me, see. Naturally he left everything to Trevor except the gamekeeper's cottage. He never thought of a little boy of six growing up to be a man of thirty and wanting a home of his own.
Meg Lack of imagination seems to run in the family. (*She bangs down side-plates*)
Hughie Now you *have* got imagination, Meg. Soon as I mentioned that cottage, you saw what could be done with it. I never thought of it.
Meg You never thought of whose land lay next door to it either, did you?
Hughie Well, I didn't because I know. It's your Uncle Gareth's.
Meg Now dead.
Hughie All gone to that daughter in Australia, I suppose. Ninety acres of good arable land.
Meg (*casually*) His *money*'s gone to her. But apparently it's difficult to send ninety acres overseas. Anyway, she's got two thousand of her own out there.
Hughie That so? What did he do with it, then?
Meg He left it to me.
Hughie What? (*Rising and coming round the front of table to Meg*) You mean to say you've got ninety acres next door to us?
Meg (*looking up at him; hopefully*) Yes, Hughie.
Hughie (*in sudden excitement*) And you tell me I've no imagination! Don't you *see*, Meg?
Meg (*lighting up*) See what, Hughie?
Hughie Trevor wants more land: you want Trevor——
Meg No, Hughie——

Hughie Trade in your land for marriage lines and you've got him!
Meg (*stamping her foot and bursting into tears*) Oh, Hughie!

Meg runs out R

Trevor enters from the back yard

Hughie Trevor, do you know what——
Trevor Get going, you. You've been hanging round this kitchen half the morning.
Hughie Just a minute, Trevor. Have you finished with Phoebe and Alice as marriage propositions?
Trevor Finished? I never started. To hell with women. I can manage without them. (*He helps himself to whisky*)
Hughie Not without Meg, you can't. And I've something to tell you about Meg that'll pull you up short.
Trevor (*coming down to the settle*) You can't tell me anything I don't know. She's a tartar, like the rest of them.
Hughie She is also the owner of Gareth Lewis's ninety acres.

Trevor chokes on his whisky

Trevor Eh? Ninety acres. He left them to *her*?
Hughie Right, Trev.
Trevor (*rising galvanically and pointing to the door*) Get out, Hughie. Get out and find something to do.
Hughie Going, Trevor, going.

Meg enters R

(*Pausing*) I'd do anything for you, Meg, anything. And you think I've no imagination!

Hughie exits into the back yard

Trevor Sit down a minute, Meg.
Meg (*brave, but brusque*) What for? You want some dinner, I suppose? (*She goes to the stove*)
Trevor Leave it. I want to talk to you.
Meg Then talk while I'm working. I'm all behind as it is. (*Calling*) Sandra! Sandra, I want you.

Trevor crosses rapidly to the door R

Sandra enters R

Trevor Be off! She doesn't want you!

Sandra vanishes

Trevor turns to Meg and seizing her by the waist, drags her over to the settle

Now listen. You are about to get the biggest surprise of your life. You're a good housekeeper, Meg, but you don't want to keep other folk's houses for the rest of your life, do you?

Meg Not particularly.

Trevor Brace yourself, girl. I'm offering you the chance to run this one as your own. Understand?

Meg No.

Trevor Dammit, woman, I'm asking you to marry me. What do you say?

Meg No.

Trevor WHAT? You haven't taken it in. Shock, I suppose.

Meg No.

Trevor (*shouting*) Curse it, what's wrong with me? I don't even smell of mothballs now.

Meg (*rising*) You smell of *greed*. First you wanted a wife with four hundred acres; then one with three hundred. Now you've come down to ninety. That's a desperate big drop Trevor, my lad.

Trevor But there's profit in it for you too. Your ninety acres join my land.

Meg No they don't. They join the boundary fence by the gamekeeper's cottage. And that's Hughie's.

Trevor (*blustering*) Hughie is my man, and that boundary's my affair.

Meg (*topping him*) Hughie is *my* man, and that boundary is ours. Sandra!

Trevor By God! So you two have been plotting behind my back, have you? I'll soon set you to rights!

Sandra enters R

Sandra Did you call?
Trevor NO!
Meg YES! Run and tell Mr Hughie to come here double-quick.

Sandra sets off towards the back door

And bring that jacket off the line when you come back.

Sandra exits through the back door

Trevor This is a put-up job. Hughie's fired! Finished! He can go and live in his gamekeeper's cottage with half an acre and see how he likes it.

Meg Understand this, Trevor. Hughie knows no more than that I've inherited Uncle Gareth's land. And his first thought was of you, not me, worse luck. He thinks I want to marry *you*, heaven help me.

Trevor But you just said Hughie is your man.

Meg He is. But the poor lad doesn't know it yet.

Trevor (*nastily*) P'raps you're not his woman.

Meg Oh yes I am. He doesn't know that either, but I'm tired of waiting for the penny to drop. He leaves it all to me ... He's coming. Do you want him to see you down and out?

Trevor I'm not down.

Meg (*pushing him towards the door* R) Only out.

Trevor is pushed off R

Hughie enters the back door, breathless

Hughie What is it? What's happened?

Meg Nothing much. (*She moves to the sink*) Dinner will be a bit late, that's all.

Hughie (*puzzled*) Why send for me early if it's going to be late? Did he ask you, Meg?

Meg Yes.

Hughie (*brightening*) So you won't be leaving?

Meg Yes, I shall.

Hughie (*dropping into his chair,* R *of the table*) But why?

Meg (*turning and coming to the table*) Because I'm not selling my ninety acres for a bit of paper that'll turn me into an unpaid housekeeper. That's why ... I'd sell to the right bidder, mind, but he's a bit slow in the uptake. By the way——

Hughie (*disconsolately spinning a knife on the table*) Yes, Meg?

Meg —you know my ninety acres run alongside the boundary fence of your land, don't you Hughie?

Hughie I suppose they do.

Meg Make a nice little farm when that cottage is done up, won't it?

Hughie (*sitting up with a jerk*) Eh?

Sandra enters from the back door with the jacket

Sandra It still pongs, but not so bad. Where'll I put it?
Meg Give it to Hughie. He'll be needing it.
Hughie That? But that's Trevor's courting jacket.
Meg That's right. You'll be needing it. Put it on and bring that bowl down to the raspberry canes.
Sandra But I've *picked* the raspberries.
Meg Don't you be dense too, my girl. Help Hughie on with that jacket. Hurry up, Hughie. I've waited long enough.

Meg exits through the back door

Sandra, smiling broadly, takes the jacket and holds it out to Hughie, who regards it owlishly. Then his face slowly lights up as comprehension dawns

Hughie Do you know what, Sandra? I believe it's me she wants. Me!
Sandra (*laughing*) Course it is, you great baby. Always has been.
Hughie (*clasping the jacket to him in ecstasy*) Oh, my lovely Meg! (*He dives into the jacket*) How do I look?
Sandra Terrible! And you smell worse. If she can take you in that thing, she must be busting with love.
Hughie (*surveying himself in the mirror above the settle*) I'm her man. Me! The second fiddle.

Trevor enters R

Trevor Where's this dinner then . . .? Here! What the hell are you doing with my jacket?
Hughie (*swaggering towards the back door*) Courtin', Trevor, courting.

Hughie picks up the bowl and exits

Sandra peals with laughter

Trevor (*shouting*) And shut up, you. Where's the dinner?

Sandra continues to laugh as——

the CURTAIN *falls*

FURNITURE AND PROPERTY LIST

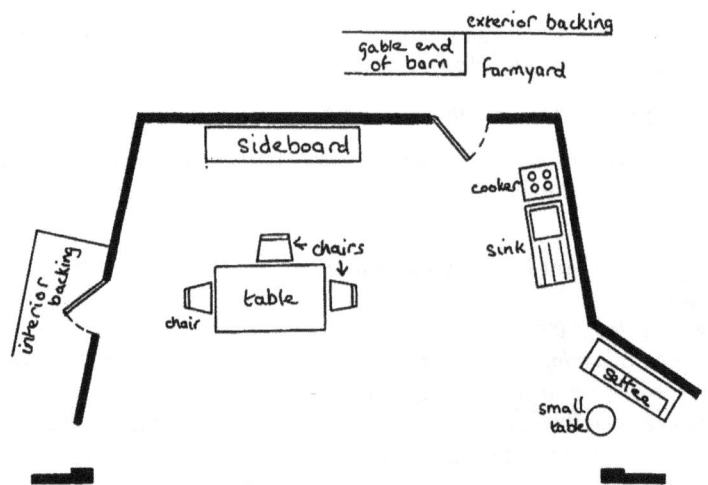

On stage: Table. *On it:* bowl of pastry, rolling-pin, flour, jam, pie-tin, bowl of potatoes, knife
3 chairs. *On one:* a newspaper
Sideboard. *In it:* cutlery, crockery, bottle of whisky, jar of instant coffee, sugar-bowl, jug of milk. *On it:* tray, bowl. *Under it:* Trevor's shoes. *In drawer:* tablecloth
Cooker (practical). *On it:* kettle
Sink and taps (practical). *In sink:* saucepans, pots
Draining-board. *On it:* teapot, tea, tea-towel
Settle
Small table
Mirror on wall above settle

Off stage: Jacket **(Meg)**
Towel, comb **(Trevor)**
Riding-crop **(Phoebe)**
Silver tray set with silver coffee set—jug of coffee, sugar-bowl, jug of milk, cups, saucers, spoons **(Meg)**

Personal: **Phoebe:** handkerchief

LIGHTING PLOT

Practical fittings required: nil
Interior. A farmhouse kitchen/living-room. The same scene throughout

To open: general interior lighting—morning
No cues

www.ingramcontent.com/pod-product-compliance
Lightning Source LLC
Chambersburg PA
CBHW070455050426
42450CB00012B/3292